MW00564719

Additional Praise for KNOCKING THE STARS SENSELESS

Clif Mason writes with a fierce beauty. In *Knocking the Stars Senseless* poems journey to real and imagined worlds over unbelievable distances through fantastic scenes. Like Wordsworth and other great 19th century writers who traveled by foot, reading these words is to inhabit a place of motion that tends to the magic of sound. This book invites us along to visit with fellow travelers, sway with the music of nightfall, and watch stars and cityscapes dazzle with lights. We might wonder where we're going in this new gorgeous book over these lines that unfold and question, skillfully playing with form. And the wonder is the pleasure, one foot, one poem, and then another."

— Laura Madeline Wiseman, author of *Velocipede* and *Drink,* and editor of *Women Write Resistance: Poets Resist Gender Violence*

Knocking the Stars Senseless is a deeply moving meditation on the contemporary world that swirls around us. Mason is unflinchingly clear-eyed about human suffering—Sandy Hook, police shootings, the incandescent evil of Auschwitz—and in so doing, he also marvels at how we hold onto each other, even as the world tries to pull us apart. Through thrumming word choice, and a keen sense of form, Mason explores the tension between life and nonexistence, the dark void above us, and the flaring stars which burn like beacons in the night. These poems celebrate such mundane chores as washing dishes and visiting a gas station, they contemplate a stuffed otter on display at a nature center, and they exhilarate at skydiving as a metaphor for life itself. Knocking the Stars Senseless is a profoundly human reflection on how we navigate the natural and built world that we are born into. Mason writes in the closing poem that, 'we are all/yes, each & every one, the last/ least, best, unexpected thing.' So it is with this collection—an unexpected thing that lingers in the imagination long after you've put it down.

— Patrick Hicks, author of *The Commandant of Lubizec* and *Library of the Mind,* and radio host of *Poetry from Studio 47*

In *Knocking the Stars Senseless*, Clif Mason works with surreal images like a magician pulling birds, stars, and waterfalls from a top hat as he waves a wand so horses and bones disappear and reappear. With a keen eye for nature and clear insight into the human experience, Mason tells a complex haunting story. We move through these dense pages—with pleasure for the victories and puzzlement and grief over terrible losses—on a whirlwind of imagery and sound as Mason drives home hard questions and unexpected truths, such as 'Is it of such small deaths our days are made?' and 'They are chanting for us all the prayers they know.' We continue on a journey filled with twists and turns, knowing this poet has the strength and care to ensure we 'come to the edge of this moment … & burn beyond all time.' This collection is guaranteed to restore the reader's belief in magic and to ignite a renewed faith in humanity.

— Cat Dixon, author of *Too Heavy to Carry, Eva,* and *The Book of Levinson*

Knocking the Stars Senseless

CLIF MASON

For more information:
Stephen F. Austin State University Press
P.O. Box 13007 SFA Station
Nacogdoches, Texas 75962
sfapress@sfasu.edu
www.sfasu.edu/sfapress

Book design: Jerri Bourrous

Distributed by Texas A&M Consortium
www.tamupress.com

ISBN: 978-1-62288-206-9

To Adrien, Vahid, Jesse, and Fred, and the memory of Jason, and to Laurie.

Contents

*Within the rock the undiscovered suns
release their light.*
—Robert Hayden

Double Narrative: This Waking Life

When I yearned for the incense of candle & canticle, I sought the
fulcrum of trance & tragedy, hawk & hook.

> The book I wrote unwrote itself as I typed. Characters
> disappeared as if kidnapped.

The wind insisted I depart, follow it across the whole planet,
honeycombed with madness & magic, derangement & delight.

> Places of importance disintegrated, as if taken apart by a soundless,
> non-violent bomb.

A friend said, *Embrace a life of intentional vagabonding, endless venturing*—& the
air began to speak in whispers & whoops, sobs & shrieks.

> Even the weather dissolved before my eyes. Clouds became cerulean.
> Tornadoes unraveled like round hay bales unrolled for the horses.

So began this waking walking life. Each day was striving without
horizon, each night rest without regret.

> Sunlight faded like stage lights going dim. Book became un-book,
> language silence.

Come along, I said. *I'd welcome the company.*

First Passage:
The Bird with Indigo Wings

Night Walk in the Republic

Owl calls on a cold night—
solemn commanding hoots.
I wander, lost, full of midnight's wanderlust.
These streets are empty & the houses dark.
I fear the return to home & bed,
a night of tormented dreams.
There has been another mass murder
in an American town.
I try to expect nothing of flesh or dust,
but I fail time & again.
I want a planet to burn with love
under the shoulder of the risen moon.
I want black squirrels to eat their fill of apples,
the horses' hooves to point always to the sea.
What do the lovers of earthshine worship
as night disintegrates?
The gleaming planet fades
& we are bereft, without breath.

We are bereft, without breath,
as the gleaming planet fades
& night disintegrates.
What do the lovers of earthshine worship—
the horses' hooves pointing always to the sea,
black squirrels eating their fill of apples
under the shoulder of the risen moon?
I want a planet. To burn. With love.
But it fails time & again.
Should I expect nothing, then, of flesh or dust
in an American town?
There has been another mass murder,
another night of tormented dreams.

I fear the return to home & bed.
The streets are empty & the houses dark,
as I wander, lost, full of midnight's wanderlust,
& command solemn hoots
from the owl calling on a cold night.

Day of the Dead

Why are so many we meet missing hands or noses,

ears or feet? Where did they go? Who collected them?

What have they done with all the fingers?

Have you found the trunk of moldering toes?

This is the age of amputation.

We learn to live with less & still less.

What can we expect when every day is the Day of the Dead?

The stars are darkened by smoke & ash. Orion is hidden.

The old monk, the moon, rows his black boat across black waters.

Ghost Music

The hard month's murders begin
without ruth or rue.
The singing tongue is cut from autumn's river,

& earth is littered with the feathers of pheasants
& of finches the size of a baby's fist.
My father flies away on a condor's midnight wings.

I can no longer read the Persian calligraphy
of honeybee flight or taste nectarines' wet red ardor.
The hives of wild honey are depleted

& milkweed pods are aerial ghost towns.
As the smoke of leaf fires leave ash in my throat,
the burning bushes & purple plum become racks

of naked antlers. The lone sumac stand that blinked
suddenly on—vermilion—in daybreak sun,
is losing its leaves, looking each morning more ragged—

jagged-edged as a box of old saws.
The sumac put on their gaudy party rags,
their tarty autumn chic, only, one last Bacchic binge

past, to cast them off again as quick & fall
into denuded desuetude.
& late roses—blushing heartsblood, crushed velvet—

all unknowing, are frost-torn despite their thorns.
Stasis of marigolds, daisies, & impatiens:
ice-speared by the impatient season.

Unwilling to let leaf or petal or father die from my eyes,
unready for such dear loss,
I stare long into October's mortuary light.

Rubbed raw by the physics of discontent,
challenged by distance & darkness.
Silence rings a bell without sound, & the echo persists,

wrapping me in ghost music, filling me with all
the thoughts I haven't been able—
or haven't allowed myself—to think before.

What happens if I re-imagine the world—
say, paintings that don't hang on walls
but float throughout the house, waves high as stars,

my father alive? What happens
if he holds wind again in his hands
& lets it roll off the ends of his fingers?

When he tastes darkness, the light in his bones
gleams. Bees stir & the hive runs
with honey. He walks from the end of one day

to another, then walk back & picks up his footprints.
In the midnight hour, nitrogen seeps into the soil.
When he kneels at the transept of wildness, in the church

of an unknown forest, does he recognize
his fellow pilgrims? No one should have to walk alone
in the witching hour, fearful daybreak will not come,

uncertain of everything but the bastinado of self-interest.
Wind picks his pocket again as he ambles.
It steals again sweat from his body, music from his ears.

It takes again the gait from his legs, taste from his tongue.
The more it steals, the less he feels bound by gravity.
He laughs as the wind bears him off like a kite.

Family Separation

The dying of an iris torments the night
& a child's pain wolfs through the room.

Her fear becomes a confusion
of black orchids, & summer's hummingbirds

die from her eyes. How long before
her heart's otter lies cold & wet,

without breath, & a dwarf star
erases the space of her body?

Clouds blacken and spread snow over her grave.

The Sea Anemone Must Wed Lightning

Long ago the stars locked the winds
into their narrow cells, the sea
into its blue print. I still feel bound

& restless, walking all day
in a sleep mask, seeking a time
when big flakes falling on pines

& birches were easy as a razor cut.
When I turn my face into a camera,
my life becomes an endless recording.

Drinking the tepid tea of approval,
I become irritable & chafe
at those limits. I hear vague commands—

Remove the stones from your eyes.
Open the windows in the house
of Song. Roll up the gates

of the reservoir of sound—
& I'm uncertain how to respond.
Hearts cut from the bodies

of blue whales & black rhinoceros
are sewn forever into the nightmares
of our children. Workers resign

themselves & creep through every street
in the city to the cemeteries of their jobs.
Material hands slowly become

unconsummated dust. On the news,
parents were arrested for putting
a shock collar on a handicapped child.

Did they later plant charred stakes
in orchards & pretend they were apple
& pear trees? Each thing is its simple self

& more. The purple martin
is a door to one of Saturn's rings.
The swan is a bolt shot

from a crossbow. This is midnight's
necropolis & all my neighbors
have found their ways to the dark

country of sleep. Perhaps even now
they walk past me in soundless
dreams. Do I pursue my own way

to the horsehead nebula under Orion's
belt? Do I pause in the radiant
chapel where death marries life?

Do I stop to see rose after rose
fall through a hole in the night?
I look into the trees' high monasteries.

The monks meditate, staring out
leafy candlelit windows, drawing
with great yearning, groundwater

up through the boles' long arteries.
In the neighborhood of a thousand dogs,
not a single bark is heard.

~

Grass succumbs to its green madness.
Its cabal of roots drinks from darkness
& plots its workers' revolution.

The street is full of gashes & clotting
blood. Time is the frieze of shadows
on clouds, the freeze of blood

at betrayal. Forgiveness, if it ever
arrives, comes hard as a club
against the temple, as a knout's

iron tongues on a bare back.
Goose cries crack open the night,
slit the moon's pockmarked skin.

If I cut my finger in the dark,
will mortality enter? Will it eat my flesh
as ineluctably as sun's golden bucket

rises from night's cold well?
What can I say of this suffering
except that it is mine? I will carry it

into autumn, holding it over
my head as, crossing a river,
I would a bundle of clothes.

One day the red horses of my blood
will gallop away & I will fall
to the stable's stone floor. Cold moonlight

will be my winding cloth. My love
will wear a ruby necklace of grief,
red drops against a black dress.

~

Walking once more at night & a star
falls into my eye & bleeds out
in garnet winks. Am I snagged

in the moon's coiling snakes? What do
these streets have to do with the world's
angry numbers, with the mechanisms

of hurt & displacement? I don't wish
to see, yet the television forces me to see,
flower gardens reduced to dust,

people crawling on broken knees.
Just so do I learn the alphabets of dread.
A kid leans against a dumpster,

a needle nailing his arm to concrete,
litter, & illegitimate sewage. A rosary
of star fragments wreathes his neck.

Blessings on those who scalpel
open sky & let daybreak intrude,
the vitreous melt of iceprick stars,

who drain the dark with well-
timed cuts & drive out its coven
of fears, who help the poor & brain-

ruined chew the black poppy, bleak
narcotic, of greatly belated, undreaming
sleep. In a home that I pass, darkness

seeps into hushed air & the room
turns blue with forsaken light. A child's
unmoving body burns sapphire.

In the dark of the moon, he has fallen
from a great height & lies half-
hidden in shadows. Where is the bird

with indigo feathers? I don't hear
his singing, calls that pierce the brain
with arrow after arrow of grief.

The star made of bones lies down
in the fields' black earth. It is planted
in the furrows like a green promise.

I want the song that will lift
the moon's white bone back
into its black socket. I want the song

in which a hundred horses will gallop
wild from Earth's green mouth,
in which wind will whirl weightless

but sovereign over vast pastures
of flowing grass. I feel the hunger
of lost stars. Five gold suns

become five gold coins become
five gold spots on an old
woman's hand. Light flowers, petal

upon golden petal. I want the song
in which water, risking all, dives over
a falls & wails all the way down.

I want the song that will raise a fallen
child, if only for a day,
an afternoon, an hour, that will startle

the infinite, unsoothing blue
with one unchristened drop
of burning gold & shatter this room.

~

The moon flings its spears against
the sea's chain mail but cannot
pierce it. I wade thigh-deep in the cold

shallows, & ghosts of the innumerable
dead throng about. Their desire
for detachment from this world

gleams like moonlight trapped
in transparent skulls, making them shine
like jellyfish. They crawl crab-wise

down the beach's cracked shells & rocks
to the water's edge, where they slither
into the waves like serpents or eels,

unable to swim more than a few feet.
They cluster, clutching for connection,
entwining for warmth. They lie about,

a writhing litter of spirits. Seeing what
I thought never to see, I stand there
stunned, stammering. They take no notice

of me, in my warm sheet of flesh, but wait
for the tide to flow out & float
or drag them across the great water.

~

Pausing in my walk—without a pen,
I write an epic. I simply point & the tale
appears, a dream written by light

in the air. It begins, *The sea anemone*
must wed lightning. April trees must leaf out
in blades. Stones must grow fins

& leap into rivers & oceans. & it ends,
The dead speak obliquely to us, in fireflies
heliographing lust on an August night,

in stars spilling, a million frog eggs
across black space, in the rose-pink cloud
haloing a bony quarter moon.

They speak in dew gems arcing grass blades
down, in the algorithm of bird flight.
These are the answers the dead make

to our questions. We need not
demand words. They're close as fingernail
to finger, eyelash to eye, heartbeat

to heart. In the whir & blur
of hummingbird wings, in lightning strike
& otter dive, in a hundred other ways

each day, they say they know
nothing of pain. Do you hear? They are
chanting for us all the prayers they know.

Broken Bells

As the world travels angry songlines of blame,
we tread sand, until the tide sounds—
horses of ice, & the mourning wrack of stars—

the ruckus & debris of shells, each a lack
in the long night's lake, filled with dirges
& forsaken dreck, the bronze mistake

of broken bells. When the glass holding the stars
shatters, shards of light strike us, slicing open
our thoughts to let the darkness inside escape.

Fugue for the Sandy Hook Dead

In the cemetery of night,
    the weeping spreads
        briars
   & brambles.
What does an assault weapon bullet
     do to a child's body?
What must we give up to count
     the entry wounds?
Earth holds their bodies.
She will treat them
    with the kindness
     she offers all of the dead,
  the kindness that asks them
     to drink from the stars' chalice
   the black anodyne of sleep.

In the cemetery of stars,
     the bodies spread
  their black brambles & briars.
What do entry wounds do
     to the earth?
What must we give up
     for the dead to count?
Weeping holds the bodies
    & offers to treat them
     with the black anodyne
  of kindness.
A child asks to drink
    from night's empty chalice.

What does the weeping do
     to bodies?

What must we give up
        for the entry wounds

                to count
      the brambles & briars?
The black anodyne of weeping

             holds the earth
   & the cemetery offers to treat

          the stars
     with the kindness
    only a child's body can know.
Sleeping assault weapon bullets

       spill from a black chalice
  & night

     asks all of the living to drink.

Knocking the Stars Senseless

                    Baton Rouge, St. Paul, Dallas, Baton Rouge

In your hands the machinery of dark,
                    in your hands the capillaries
          of light.
A thunderhead of flies
                    burns out
                              of the city's skull
          & buries the moon.

The zodiac of familiar stars
                              is erased—
          replaced by the glacier's red
                              ache,
               the screaming of clouds,
          the asterisked note
                    that overtakes the text of the hour.

Voices freeze on tongues,
                    words break
                              on the tips of teeth.
Flowers wilt
                    & leaves wither
                              & fall.

The earth has had enough.

It has tired of us
                    & no longer wants to support us.

Of course, it does support us.

The earth has a green nobility

                        we can't fathom,

                                a green forgiveness.

We feel only the bolting horse,

                 the grizzly bear slap,

                         the cardiac arrest.

The stars' fury

              fractures

                     the ragtime tune.

Whatever it is we dream of doing,

           we are helpless

                 not to let the news undo.

Perhaps someone will write

          a lean

                 & lonesome blues

                       to temper

           these distempered times.

Can you hear that song,

                      withholding

      the insult to judgment,

              knocking the stars

                   senseless,

        & making this untuned rage

           newly tuneful?

You hold the notes in your hands.

Release them.

After the Political Speeches

The stone is an abacus counting the cost of breathing.

Each bird's heart is attached to an electric wire.
We kneel in gasoline-drenched sawdust.
Do you seek the forgiveness of glass.
If the streets are empty, the time may have passed.
Boxes of photographs are stacked at the curb.

The act of careless consequence is fatal.

The tree drops its last apple.
The falcon kills its last mouse.
The elevator makes its last descent.
The television broadcasts its last show.
The phone sends its last text.

Inside the collapsed mine is a ring of gold.

Without flowers hummingbirds die.
Without rivers earth ravines & rends itself.
Without voice people become feckless as ghosts.
Without dreams sleep becomes death.
Without psalms the dead walk with the dead.

If anyone felt desire, the wind would blow again.

Depression

A green amnesia incites even as it dulls all thought
& sense into a sleep that is not sleep.
All my mirth pours out—showers of silver & gold,
sapphires & rubies—& my desires become
arid as Namibia's Skeleton Coast, with its vast haul
of whale & seal bones & wrecked ships.

All the harvesters are falling apart, shaking & shuddering
& collapsing before they can leave the fields.
All the luxury automobiles are falling apart,
in garages & shops & on the street.
All the bridges & skyscrapers are falling apart,
falling to rust & poisonous dust & bent & sheered rebar.
All the planes are falling apart, right in mid-air,
falling apart & streaking in pieces from the sky.
All the roses & daisies & chrysanthemums
are falling apart, even those still locked in the bud.
All the crickets & cicadas are falling apart,
their exoskeletons dissolving around them,
silencing them like radios switched off.
All the ocean waves are falling apart,
littering the sand with shells & jellyfish & squid,
falling apart, shifting in liquid silk
& satin, deliquescing, disappearing.
All the vocations are falling apart, breaking & shattering
& vanishing, leaving everyone with nothing to do.

Ashes sift from birds' wings & the leaves of trees.
Ashes fall from the clouds & the crowns of skyscrapers.
Ashes slip from tongues & lips & the corners of eyes.
Ashes rain from the pelts of foxes & wolves,
of lions & deer & giraffes.

Ashes grease the bearings of trains & trucks,
of automobiles & airplanes.
Ashes escape from the guts of every other machine.
Ashes spill from the bodies of every human
on the planet & from the ghosts of every human
who's left the planet.

It's a time of broken helicopters & aluminum forests,
of vacant cinemas & disordered dreams,
of rust & riots, rampages & impulse purchases,
of malarial fevers & red planet hallucinations,
of sleep & sleeplessness, question & quandary,
of panic on the pulse & seizures in the body politic,
of winds knocking whole islands into darkness
& streets raging with water,
of charisma & curiosity, caricatures & karaoke,
of the regretting of everything
& the regretting of nothing,
of the resisting of nothing
& the resisting of everything,

It's a time of too early & too late,
of time beyond time & of time without time.

It's a time of 12-tone scales & tone-deafness,
of Elvis impersonators & impresarios of impermanence,
of happiness for all & happiness for none,
of the brazenness of the billy club
& the bravado of the bowling league,
of tent cities & subtexts of subtexts,
of selfies for everyone & selfies for no one,
of rough drafts & final drafts.
It's a time of the renaissance of everything
& the renaissance of nothing.

It's a time of too early & too late,
of time beyond time & of time without time

My love requests a sweeter torte, a less tart tart.
But I can serve up only this farrago of flame, rust,
& plutonium fighting dogs, a slurry of old razors
& broken binoculars.
We walk the street of personas,
in a city of ambiguous intentions.
The air is rank with theater, humid with deceit.
Someone steals the plans for the resurrection
of the feather duster.
My love seeks filigree but I can offer only famine
& fallacy, the failure of halogen bulbs,
the collapse of gentrified buildings.
Shopping malls pretend to be waterfalls
& waterfalls pretend to be war monuments.
When they cast the runes for the divining of skulls,
we have a star's red-rimmed eyes.
Our breaths are so shallow they aren't really breaths.
If a breath is a ghost, these are ghosts of ghosts.

Blessings upon the parable of the protozoa,
blessings upon the elegy of the egalitarian,
blessings upon the opposition of preachment
& parchment.
Blessings upon the hippogriff & giraffe,
blessings upon the garrulous & garbled,
blessings upon the inchoate & the coeval.
Blessings upon those deserving of blessings
& those undeserving,
blessings upon those rich in rewards
& those preternaturally poor,
blessings upon blessings, & anti-blessings,
& counter-blessings.

Do we feed the pigeons of our secrets?
Immersed in wet sequins, we swim in the jeweled braids
of river currents, as through a prism of disquietude.
We sail under the tattered flags of danger & daring,
dispatched to the Spice Islands of peril & panic.
When we become shadow to jade, air to star,
we loose the horse of the voice, set it free to gallop
down muddy paths, in unknown forests.
The words it sings are obscure
as the ideograms of Linear A.

That voice becomes faint & fades, but another is heard,
a voice like flying fish skimming ocean waves.
When I hear her words, I am swept off the Kaieteur Falls,
& I drop in that vertical river. We must avow & own
the falling apart, or we cannot arise from our bed of earth
& build the world again, arise & make it new.

Subdivision Eclogue

At the summit of this neighborhood's
                         highest hill,
approachable by four paths,
     leading in from four separate streets,
                        is this playground:
           jungle gym, merry-go-round,
       swings, & a tornado slide—
enough to make our three year old happy
                 the short time we'll stay.

Walking uphill, we see women & men
    giving lush grass its weekly shaving,
                 laying out sprinklers,
       edging lawns, trimming hedges,
& planting a new tree, a pin oak.
     It stands up straight as a flagpole
               in the front yard,
the big dirtball encasing its tangle of roots
       still wrapped tight in gunnysack cloth.

We see others planting in little garden plots
   & washing cars,
       as kids play whiffle ball,
glide down the streets on skateboards & bikes,
         & play basketball, one-on-one.

Atop the hill, I push our youngest in his swing,
& once he has reached his apogee of possibility,
                  I kick off, too,
     lean back, pump higher,
until I can see over the bar,
       five miles at least into the country.

Stands of cottonwoods along the Papio Creek
deepen with shade,
                    & chorus frogs chant
                                        by the thousands
                    in the run-off stream
        that makes the subdivision's mazy southern boundary—
                    chant their locust-like, throbbing song.
        Sometimes,
                            eerily,
                                        they all stop at once.
        Minutes pass,
& then, sonorously,
                    slowly,
                            they all start up again.

        One might complain about the life we live here—
that shelves in most of these houses
                                        hold more DVDs than books.
        Still, we have known darkness:
                                        a teenage girl raped,
        a boy kidnapped, his body found weeks later,
                    stripped, with multiple knife wounds.

        So, be forbearing if we seem to spend our time vainly
watching movies on big-screen TVs,
                                        or swinging our children high as we can,
        before earth pulls them down again.

Insomnia

Night is the owl's kingdom.
Wind lifts the lovers' hair
& blood pours like grief
from one chamber of the heart to another.
The moon is a pearl-handled revolver,
night a black satin coffin liner.
If the clouds were to break & the stars appear,
sleep might come to both the living & the dead?
The owl rules the world of shadows & hazard.

If the owl ruled the world of shadows & hazard,
might sleep come to both the living & the dead?
When the clouds break & the stars appear,
night becomes a black satin coffin liner,
the moon a pearl-handled revolver.
From one chamber of the heart to another
blood pours like wind
& grief lifts the lovers' hair.
Night is the owl's kingdom.

Second Passage:
The Languages of Snails
& Minerals

Kwik Shop Epiphany

Night came, a wounded bat into the oil-
stained Kwik Shop parking lot, fell down among
the Styrofoam drink-cups, & for all its toil
could not rise again on its hairy wings.
As I pumped gas into my car's ever-
ravenous tank, kids sat on the hoods of half
a dozen cars, smoking, laughing, never
once doubting that this muggy moment was life.
Their radios black-jacked the air with bass
& rapping rhymes fell, bleeding, to their knees.
One kid said he'd kick another kid's ass
if he saw him. His girlfriend smiled, said, "Please."
I washed insect-streaked windows, headlights, paid.
Was it of such small deaths our days were made?

Darkfall

For centuries we seeded the cemeteries.
So it was no surprise the soil
grew nothing but headstones.
Our hands held bleak acres of newsprint,
black bouquets of tortures & rapes,
& rapes as the instrument of torture.

Now time runs back into the machinery
of stars, eats itself like words dissolving
under the steady force of a delete key.
Now everything dies before it can occur.
No one laughs for fear of sanctioning
the sun's red bowl of hydrogen,

the incendiary bubble boiling,
blowing a typhoon of horses
& white flames, scalding & scarifying,
until passion's scarred arteries
become the cracked old crockery
of long-dead riverbeds.

In the lunar eclipse,
a murder was committed.
The murderer was unaware he was blind,
his eyes black as blasted lakes.
He was unaware that each new street
he walked was a grave.

Black sledges brought the dead
across the white wastes.
A lone voice keened like a lantern.
The air was full of harsh smoke,

I placed half dollars on the victim's
staring eyes to calm the river's

roiling waters, black as oil sludge,
that the betrayed might cross to peace.
We disrobed for the last time,
stepped out of cold skins,
& became the last light
disappearing in the river's current.

Her Art

The sky was the black of necrotic flesh.
Amid broken concrete slabs & shattered
glass, rabbits still bred. Strolling the streets
between vagrancy & vertigo, she stopped
in an alley to watch night open like a vast
chrysalis & bring mutant insects
into the world. Chemicals diffused into air
& water made bodies blacken like mold-
covered walls. As the moon's dead cylinder
floated off, blue light poured down
the mountain & rolled off horses' backs
like steam. It filled the spaces between trees
& immured campers like volcanic ash.

She wanted the horse with teeth like stars,
with a mane & tail like the fall of snow.
Its back was broad as a blue whale's,
its feet fleet as a cheetah's. Its hooves echoed
like talking drums. She called but it heard
sorrow clinging like mistletoe to her voice
& wouldn't come. She called again, this time
with a tone clear as a river of subterranean
water. The horse neighed & cantered
across night's pastures to her side.
She knew, whatever her grief, she must sing,
though her song scalded the eyes, sing,
though it boiled the heart in its bloody cauldron.

Skydiving & the Body

Drifting under parti-
colored parachutes,
we float & fly,
surveying the land,
taking in what there is to see.
We learn that parachutes

don't stop snow or ice,
war or disease.
They offer no protection
from dirty bombs or Sarin gas,
heartbreak or regret.

They keep us buoyant on air
for the time we need to make the choices we make.
They don't guarantee good judgment.
We can as easily make bad choices

as good.
We drift, thrill to the air streaming,

cold & bracing,
past our faces—
through weddings & birthdays,
careers & funerals.
We glide into illness & health,

into every version
of victory & defeat.
We almost convince ourselves
we're not sliding down at all.
Surely we exist in some all-forgiving stasis,
forever suspended in vibrant air.
We deceive ourselves, believe our lives
are the dreams of some other, sleeping self.
Or that from restless sleep we've wakened into dream.

The flint spark of fear:
When did the ground get so close?
Struggling fiercely to rise again,
we see with impossible clarity
each speedily approaching detail.

I Wore the Night Like a Roquelaure

Jade dusk held its dirk to my neck,
& I wondered at my face, disassembled
in the river's glass. The streetlights

came on & I could see the blood
spilled that day. Tattoos wore bodies
in public, & after midnight

all of our piercings left our flesh to gather
around steel drum fires under railroad
bridges. Days hemorrhaged bad luck

& regret, & nights were full of seizures
& gangrene. When moonlight mixed
with the chemicals of danger & dying,

I breathed them straight into my brain.
As the sky hid its million coins & grief
became the risen sun, opening its veins

& filling the east with blood,
every house was dressed in flowers
as drained of color as a fear-struck face.

A friend noticed my hundred wounds
but didn't see I had a brazier of red
embers in my mouth, didn't suspect

my heart, wrapped in the moon's arms,
was a portal to the sea. The aimless
stroll of a beetle consumed me,

& I crawled fifteen miles inside
the root system of an oak. Spooked
wasps spilled like bullets from papery

nests high in the house eaves, angry,
with no visible target. As trucks
pulled up to street corners & stopped,

crowds gathered & workers scurried
to hand out supplies of blame.
Don't push, there's enough for everyone.

My life was a broken cup. I'd glued
together the pieces as best I could,
but some were missing. It was unlikely

they'd be found? When I went to sleep,
I had a complete set of bones & a full suite
of muscles, but then it was harder to move

& I was not so sure. I'd lost
what I'd gained, & I'd lost fortunes
I never had. Things walked into my life

like a bear into a city street, caused
a commotion—& left just as quickly.
I was amazed they kept showing up.

If there were a limit to what a person
could lose, I hadn't found it.
Abundance was loss & loss, abundance.

~

I wanted the heart of a great horse,
churning ironworks, sun-combusting city,
& the moon, singing a song with comets

in its heart, a song so hot it could ship
icebergs into boiling currents & roil them
until they vanished. As the land came striding

down to the sea, the ocean chopped
the light into a thousand dull gunmetal
glints, & the waves attacked the shore

rocks, shifting those that would submit,
smashing themselves to watery pieces
on those that would not. As waves struck,

I yearned for the sobbing chant
of chorus frogs, faithful monks wakened
for matins, or the slow bold unfolding

of spring roses, spiraling up trellises,
each flower a red-blooming caduceus.
I yearned to speak the languages

of snails & minerals, to become
a tall candle, ablaze with blackness,
never losing wax or wick, & to walk

on a field of knives, stagger through
a forest of gibbets, & fall into the earth,
& rise up flaming, with a coronet of stars.

~

Ocean's green voice, full of delicate mist,
wound with moss & soft vegetal light.
Moon shattered & fell hissing

into the waves. What did I do when I found
myself amputated from my feet, cut off
& left to bleed into a vase of cold water?

Ocean's blue voice, full of quartz & sky.
A hundred miles of rain flung itself
back into swollen clouds. Fireflies

felt frost's distant needle & dropped,
greeny-glowing, into dying grass.
Flowers pulled back into spare, dry seeds.

Ocean's red voice, discordant with pox
& flamethrower rage, with torrential blood.
I trembled, afraid to answer.

Ocean's black voice, choked with mold
& mud & grave-earth decay.
I knew if I didn't answer, I would die.

Tongue swollen & raw, lips bloody,
my voice cracked & ragged—still I sang
in my broken voice like a dying gull,

sang of longing, a nest of thirsty roots,
gorgon-snaking down into beach sand,
sang for those who woke & found

themselves severed from their feet,
but got up anyway & walked
straight into the moon's burning mouth.

~

The sea could not rest, as I could not rest.
I swam all day, & when I tired,
turtles carried me on their hard carapaces.

They swam steadily through immense
schools of phosphorescent fish,
through moonlight laying its ice

on black waves. When the turtles left me
on a beach, the waves scraped shell
against shell, & I walked inland,

beneath the sun & beneath the moon.
Even the dead did not rest.
They were impelled, as I was impelled,

as everything was impelled, even veins
of gold in earth's deep grave.
The dead were searching,

as I was searching. The journey took me,
as the eagle took the fish, as the speechless
bride took the spellbound groom.

& when I found something, say,
a flake of micaceous rock, a broken
antler, a question mark caterpillar,

its orange spikes jagged as coral yet soft,
or a catalpa leaf, big as a Victorian
lady's fan, it was not an end.

It was never an end. The small became
vast & the vast became impossible
to deny. I could not turn away.

I could not rest, as the sea could not rest.
Rose petals fell to earth, feathers floated
in the wind. I could not rest.

~

Wherever I went, I heard sounds just past
the bounds of clarity, like leaves in wind,
like waves on a beach. No, like none

of those, more like words, new & strange
as starlight in a cave, & lovely as flower
heads cupped with rain. Everything I wanted

but didn't need drifted away, cottonwood
seeds in the breeze. My hands were lit
from within, twin lamps. Ancient birdsong

clamored in my blood, the sun leaped,
a red leopard, into morning's branches,
& my face took shape in the river water.

I wore the night like a roquelaure,
& a new song began in my head,
a song more gorgeous even than grief.

In the lark's cadence I heard it,
in the moon's steel chalice I saw it.
It drove the pistons of the jazz trumpeter's

heart, & when age leeched strength
from the grandmother & drug
her groundward, it became the meteor

in her legs, the new star of resolve
in her brain's core. The song became
the leaf locked in the bud, the flower

chained in the bulb, the dance frozen
in the stone. It became the steel filing
in the coral snake's eye, the ivy's lean arms

lifted toward the sun. The song said yes,
& whole countries were dressed
in spring's green sari, said yes,

& I swam a hundred leagues through
warm currents, said yes, & I climbed
the steps toward morning's open door.

Fugue: Assassins & the Dead

Spain 1936

Assassins walk a moonless path,
toward homes without light.
The dead dwell

in waters so cold
even stars
do not appear in them.

Assassins inhabit water so black
no light can escape it.
The dead walk toward homes
to which all power
has been cut.

Assassins walk in starless dark,

so cold
they cannot be touched.
The dead lie on a moonless path,
bringing grief to still air.

Assassins dwell in a dark

more dark
than their brains'
ruined palaces.
The dead walk untouched
on live power lines.

Assassins walk, homeless,
under frozen waters.
The dead lie cold
on a path
of golden stars.

For García Lorca

They shot him at dawn
& the sky, the earth, the very air,
became full of wounds.
His brain's cask of cut diamonds
darkened. But what gardeners
were the assassins! What roses
did they grow in Lorca's breast!
For the people's blood
ever sprang up in roses,
& the blood of the poet
was attar of rose. He lay robed
in his blood, embowered in roses,
each drop, each unwritten word,
a bloom. Rose thorns pierced
the assassins' flesh, put out
their eyes. Roses climbed
through their ribs' trellises,
spiraled round their necks.
Roses speared into jaws, split
crania. Roses shot from noses
& mouths, thrust out of ears.
Every room where his poems
were read, every theater
where his plays were performed,
instantly rivered with roses,
& the cantinas where people
recited or sang his verses
became arbors raging
with roses, crushing
breakers of blossoms.
People who brought his lines
to mind staggered drunk

on the incense of rose. His books
became beds of everblooming
roses, & Granada became
a garden city, a dark labyrinth
of roses. They dropped his body
into an unmarked grave,
& no sooner had they shoveled.
on the dirt & lime,
than a white horse galloped off
into a blood-red wind.

Lorca's Gypsies at Auschwitz

Three cars of Gypsies were attached to a train of Jews. It was mid-January & they had no way to make a fire in the over-crowded car. A father woke the second morning to the parading drone of the wheels & to blood-congealing air. He felt for his son's face—stone beneath his fingers. Black owls raked & razored his brain.

At Warsaw they were ousted. He refused to leave his boy behind but a soldier put a pistol to his head—icy "o"—& shouted at him to exit the train or stay with his son forever. He wished later he'd let the soldier blast his life against the car's boards. But something broke in him—guitar strings snapping. He kissed his boy & walked to the open door.

Their lives of endless journeying ended abruptly at the camp. The smell's insult to the nose was inescapable. His wife & daughter were yanked into another line. They screamed & he fought—until a guard raised his rifle & ordered him to stop. As he was hurried away, real snow began to fall with the other.

Over the next months, ravenous crows pecked at them with flinty beaks. They pecked at muscles, at hearts & spines. At night the Gypsies dreamed of black feathers. When the flesh was gone, they decided to gas the bones.

The crematory's white unconsecrating flames ate what the crows had not.

The Sunlight Was Mortal

Zyklon B was the most marvelous solvent.
It ate away the fabric of language, dissolved words
before they could form in the throat,
take shape on the tongue.
Words choked to death before they reached the lips.
The prisoners' mouths became words' cemeteries,
their teeth, words' monuments.
The air they breathed was mortal.
The sunlight was mortal.

On the flatbed truck, they were silent.
There was nothing to say.
The prisoners knew where they were headed
A few moments more & they would walk
the crowded streets of the underworld.
Then they climbed down from the truck
& trudged toward the gas chamber.
Desnos knew he must speak or die.
Speak *&* die.

He seized the thin hand of a woman prisoner,
mimed with utter conviction the reading of her palm,
Oh, I see you have a very long lifeline!
& you are going to have three children!
Everyone stopped, startled at the outburst.
Desnos turned & seized a man's bony hand,
tracing with forefinger the lines of his palm,
exclaimed, with great zest,
For you, too, I see a long life! Yes! & many children!

The guards looked confused.
Prisoners crowded round, offering their hands.

Desnos grasped one after another, predicted with relish
Long life! Many children! Great joy!
The guards could not make their tongues work.
They ordered everyone onto the truck,
turned around, & drove back to the barracks.
Desnos the poet had pole-axed reason.
Nobody died that day.

Ballad of the Witch

There was a held breath, a hunger of forms;
a floating that was flying, a stillness
that was infinite speed. A witch appeared
over a dune, & the sky flew off,

as if from wind shear. Light splintered
& spiked through, & words filled
her brain & breast, raced down arms
& thighs. Words shot up her spine

& coiled about ankles & feet. A green
wave struck a white cliff & a whirlwind
scattered endless petals. From everywhere
she heard birdsong & the rustling of feathers.

Wherever she turned, she saw the green
stirring & sprigging of stems & stalks,
blades & leaves. Glaciers gleamed
like incandescent bulbs, & rolling out fast

& away, a blue ocean & a billion
swimming fish. She glided clean above
coral's red dream, rose with the next hot
wave, blood salt, felt it crest beneath, then

fall, suspended far over, & smash
in clamor, crush, & incensed froth—
the heady smell of life ever born from,
borne by, death. The witch heard a lone

voice singing, & she was inside
that voice, & all she knew was song.

Wind rustled hair & people heard
the clattering sound of a thousand leaves.

The witch's mind was a green tendril
snaking from the seed, a tough woody sprout
that would never die, but grow & grow.
When she strolled through the forest,

saplings sprang from her footprints.
She could do more. She touched a tree
& blossoms popped from every twig.
When she opened her mouth in song,

leaves dressed every bough, & under
her hands broken limbs knitted themselves
to the tree again. Her incantations
raised forests from sawdust.

The witch spoke the holy tongue
of photosynthesis—the rituals simple
& few—the exchange of minerals
& water, the conversion of light

to leaf. All verbs were green
& all nouns clear silver. She grew
myrtle to bring good luck, & she wore
meadowsweet & sprigs of mistletoe

for protection. In her green home,
she drank a marigold infusion & rubbed
mugwort on mirrors for clairvoyance.
Snowflakes fell like albino cherry blossoms.

The witch gathered shadows
& tied them with twine, like sheaves.

When the horses of daylight galloped away,
she held tiny clusters of stars in her hands.

As clouds hidden inside snow banks
gossiped in soft voices, field mice dragged
their agony behind them like broken tails,
& she prepared to hang naked willow

boughs like snakes on the full moon's skull.
Did she forget what hadn't happened?
Birds ate twice their weight in sound,
trees waved great root fans below the earth,

& foxes leaped into snow, emerging
with mouths full of questions.
They bound the witch's wrists
& marched her to the pyre. The flames

rose to ankles. The fire burned off
her dress & crawled up unwilling thighs.
She screamed at the violation, stared hard
at trees, as if willing bare boughs

to bud. Her hair ignited & she wore
a headdress of fire. The last things
scorched eyes saw were apple boughs,
erupting like star giants, yes,

with leaves, exploding with blossom.
After the inferno, her lover held her
in a delicate embrace, until his aorta's pulse
smashed at her heart's ashes & she fell

away, a black mist in a freezing wind.

[In the undisclosed time before my death]

In the undisclosed time before my death
Lord, let me make one strange little poem—
not deranged, not endangered,

only strange—a poem that re-shapes
& –fashions what we thought we knew
of the world—so that a tender cupping

of a cheek in a hand becomes a slap
so hard it leaves a white handprint
where the blood has drained away

in the shape of fingers,
or the opposite—a violent slap
becomes the sweetest caress—

or the books forgotten become
the very books loved & ingrained
in memory—or the glaring hateful stare

of a person we don't know
becomes the starry-eyed glance
of the beloved—or the bunny rabbit

bolt after the Great Dane—
or, or, or—yes, one strange little dream
of a poem, in which I need not worry

about death, but can wander forever
in the sunny countryside of your love—
or in which you simply lean into me,

place your lips on mine,
& stop the impulsive flood of words
with a no less impetuous kiss.

Housework

There is a specious peace in dishwashing—
a transient release from daily cares
in the cloudy bank of soap bubbles flashing
prismatically—a small truce in the wars,
both great & small, of living in the world.
Oh, but to sink one's hands into the warm
water, to swish it round & feel it swirled
over one's fingers, is to know the storm
of frets abated, to feel that sweet, sudden
comfort that rises up arms & descends
upon the heart—is to want to be sodden
forever. But there is the catch that sends
ice into the water: I can't stop time.
Still, I can feel the more—& yet make my rhyme.

Third Passage:
Night of Saws & Brocade
& Stolen Dreams

Ocean of Incomparable Light

Petals fall all night from the trees,
pieces of palpable moonlight.
Toads hop through the grass

and frogs evangelize
from the runoff creek.
Everywhere is the dripping of leaves,

trees shimmering and shivering.
Star water falls in bright droplets.
Night presses, trying to suppress light,

but light defies the oppression.
Time does not abandon us—
or our prayer for a modest tenure

on the earth. We are emboldened
by this ocean of incomparable light
& we are anointed with the oil

of a star's beneficent dream—
beacon of the vast water
we cannot help but see as home.

When Dreams Become Porous

When I speak
    the familiar tongue
        of inconsistency,
   when I hold darkness
    like a lamp in my hand,
   when the stars
      hallucinate,
           having drunk
     some green distillate
of wormwood
      & shredded
        their synapses—
I burn, an immolation suicide,
        in the House of Lies.

In the tent of mist—
         intent on planets,
      dream fragments,
   figments of ancient passions—
          fire veils
     blind me,
   flame vapors
       pierce me.
Not even my ghosts recognize me.

When the queen
    of daylight's empery
      is born anew
  & my pulse hammers
       in my wrist
   & I can't catch my breath,
         moments lost

                    resurrect
in a foggy mirror.

When the window becomes porous,
                    the stone becomes porous
          & the tree becomes porous,
                              & when the tree
                    becomes porous,
          the light rips right through the bark,
                              right through its roots.
                    & when the root tips
                              become tender
                    & porous,
          light streams into the soil,
          & the light shines right through
                              the worms & grubs,
          & gophers & moles,
                              right through snakes & rabbits
                    & the low-frequency dreams
of all the sleepers in their houses.

When dreams become porous,
                              skulls & spines
                    light up
          like city blocks at night,
                    & thoughts become porous,
          & lovers become porous,
                    until there is no longer
                              any edge or boundary,
          until skin is porous to skin,
& blood is porous
                    to blood,
                              & time itself
                    is porous,
          & the earthly shell of all things

                              becomes porous
          with the radiant

                                              now

                    & now

                         & now.

The Otter

at the Ak-Sar-Ben Aquarium

I am startled at the fervor
that must have been its life,
to seem,
even in death,
stuffed, so vital.
Its fur is a dusky brown,
the hairs thick,
coarse,
silently radiant--
silver along the throat.
It must have been
black & sleek
in the river water--
faster than fish,
swimming down
rainbow
& brook trout,
despite dartings,
twistings,
rococo circlings.
More often
it was so crafty,
so swift a fisher,
it would strike them
broadside,
before they could shift
a fin.
Ears & nose
valved against water,
it corkscrewed,
then cannoned,

through the current,
long tail
ruddering behind.
Backwards,
forwards,
it swam both ways
with equal ease,
equal grace.
& it moved better
on land than skunks
or badgers--
ran better than raccoons.
More playful than a cat,
it was eager
to coast down rapids,
or leaping,
folding forelegs in,
to sled down
a snowbank
& out in a slide
onto the ice.
But now here it stands:
poised on a log,
webs showing
between wide-
fanned toes,
thick tail curving
to a
point,
whiskers bristling
like straws from its face.
Brown taxidermist's eyes
stare fiercely,
forever,
at the opposite wall.

It has just emerged
from the river.
It is scanning the trees
for a sound
it heard
when the bullet rips
through its belly
& it rolls into the mud,
body slinky as a snake's,
its ears still hearing
that gunshot--
but permanently deaf
to the words
& noises
of the tourists.

Summer Nocturne

Moon a salmon-rose scimitar,
sky blue-black as stone.
Dusk-enshadowed oak boughs,
black leaf folded on
black leaf—
lit by an owl's eyes—
gold gem-fire.

A raccoon waddle-wades,
slugging its belly through tall,
dew-glinting ditch grass,
while a possum,
thinking itself invisible,
slips, like a fireman,
down a cottonwood bole.

Horses stand, dead-dozing,
in a pasture,
as crickets sheer leg metal
from all sides.
Chorus frogs sob-chant
spring's breed-lust,
unending mind-benumbing wail,
& bats' bony wing-leather
whirs above,
tiny propellers.

When headlights slice white
across night,
everything bestills.
A beetle the size of a quarter
makes a determined creep

                                    across the asphalt,
                        until it is drenched
in full, blind, heatless light.
                    The car passes,
                                        missing the beetle,
                    & darkness returns,
wrapping all in its cape of peace.

A Handful of Fireflies

When day brims with derelicts
                              & dire bears,
                  overflows with incantations
& strange charms,
                  we learn again:
                        to choose is to appraise
            & appreciate—
                        the bullfrog's bravado
& the cricket's charisma,
                                    the fox's glamor
                  & the rabbit's radiance.

When wind puts on
                                    the clothes of clouds,
                  we can see it,
as if for the first time,
                              just as the voice utters words
to give it shape & dimension.
            The voice shifts & spins
                              & rolls airy boulders
                  across the sky.

On the other side of the planet,
                                    people perish
                  in the uranium forest,
while in cities here,
                  murder is smeared
            across every building's paper face.
            What do the gold filaments
in the eyes of carved idols
                              know of this pain
                  that cuts like a saber of frozen ink?

The river rolls its long body over,

                                      black as the belly

                 of a rotting carp.

Nothing can bathe in it & be cleansed,

nothing can drink from it & live.

        The river is the ghost

                               of an Arabian horse,

             stars the calls of hungry owls.

There is no wind,

                            as there is no air.

        Everyone is suffocating,

                         both the living

& the no longer living,

           who are not yet dead.

My love tosses

                           a handful of fireflies

               into black sky,

to burn as close to forever

                         as we can imagine.

        I plant pines & spruce,

                  scrub oak & birch,

             Chinese ideograms,

to be read right to left.

She squeezes out dense clouds

                                 like dishrags,

             making lakes & creeks

               & rivers & puddles.

        I clap a million shells

to a million worms,

             & insects skitter

                    in all directions.

My love takes films

        of everything she's done

    & edits them

into dreams.

    I create love between humans,

& just to give everything

       an edge,

           I invent sex.

    She slings dust into afternoon air

        & birds take wing—

     feathered words.

    I take bells & flutes

& instruments of every kind

       & set them in the throat

     to sing.

    My love seizes words,

        orders them

      in ecstatic ways,

   & speaks

     the first poems.

Walking the Dog

Small flakes still fell,
sticking in the dog's long coat.
An owl chanted its *koan*.
& cold peppered my face.
Fresh snow grumbled beneath my boots.

Leaf Ballad

Never dreaming I an the whole tree,
much less the forest. Yet knowing,
without me, both tree & forest

would be less, would not be
what they might have been,
& should be. The tree

is a green force, & I am within
the force, a way for the force to be.
I am needed, just as all

leaves are. For, without
the leaf, there is no tree,
no forest, no force at all.

The sun loves us & we return
the love. Without love,
there is no leaf, & the other way

around, too. A leaf is something
of import. One in billions
All the billions in one.

October Butterfly

Red leaves on the tree:

                                         a book whose words & pages

                 vanished

                           as I read.

A regal fritillary flits

             through this tree stand,

                         a ferocity

                                 of leaf-fire orange

                 against cloudy day,

                               black-dashed

                     & dotted above

     (hyphens embroidering

                     wingtips)

                                   & studded,

             almost spattered,

       with gray-silver orbs

                           below.

It staggers through air,

                       flinging itself forward,

        by mercurial fits

                                 side to side,

               but abruptly

                             plunging,

           then just as suddenly

    jerking

                       upward,

          reeling,

       careering,

                     speeding forward

         by starts,

                                        feints, falters,
                        near stops,
        all the while breathing in
                                    great gulps & gasps
                    of oxygen
        through its abdominal air vents,
                            its compound eyes
                                                    seeing
                with brain-dazing,
                                    -dizzying giddiness:
                    turning leaves
        (constantly, casually loosed from boughs,
                                spinning down in freefall,
                often in butterfly's direct path,
                                        spiraling down
                    into Everything),
                                    grasses brown,
                    browning,
        & yet green,
                            last late flowers,
                                                    poet,
                & dry-brittle weed stalks,
                                    hollowing—
        all the spiny spokes, braces,
                                battlements,
                                    flying buttresses,
                pinnacles, piers, & parapets
        of their architectures—
                                                I say,
                its thousand-&-more-faceted eyes
                        transmitting to this flyer
                    in a furor
        a landscape shattered,
                            shredded,
                                sheered,

                                   pieced,

        sliced,

                  fragmented—

    but stupefyingly,

                  this profusion of shards

           & frames of light arriving

                                        sorted,

                        cross-filed,

              righted, & fused

        as a single seamless color picture.

The regal flits fast,

                                reverses itself,

                floats,

    thrusts somewhere on,

                    somehow never

           striking bark knuckles

                on trunks & branches,

    somehow never diving,

                  quite,

                      into earth.

Not yet.

The thistles it sucked nectar from,

                  tasting with its sensitive feet,

    are dead or dying.

The regal has long since sky-danced

           (pranced, preened,

                          careered,

    seeking with greedy crazed grace)

                        & mated—

        in those first vertiginous hours

           after it crept wetly forth from chrysalis,

        dried extended wings

                silken-soft,

& their sex scales began

                                    to perfume the air about

         with pheromones.

Still I think it is some kind of love

                           that propels

     this creature through this cloudy,

                               cool

             October day,

      that sends it lurching

                       between trees,

        between grass & heavy heavens.

& that love, as I imagine it,

                 will keep regal

                          upright

             & flying,

        seeking,

seeking—

    until in a surprised ultimate moment

                      it is death-frost

          -stunned,

its hard-beating wings,

            shocked,

                         stop

       mid-stroke,

            it submits,

& plummets forever

         into ever-receiving,

     ever-persisting earth.

The Old Crow

       Even in full moonlight
I cannot see
           the old crow
in the tree at night,
               head tucked
under a wing.
       Yet I know it is there,
a blackness
           robed in blackness.

Every Awakening Was a Hunger

We climbed the rungs of the mountain's stair
but the indignities of this world still found us.
Dismay & delight still wore each other's clothes.

Wolves carried insomnia deep into the night,
so deep no light could find them.
As cold winds ghosted through wind chimes,
they left invisible fingerprints on the windows' glass
& aged the bones of the house.

How far did we walk with the giant dog of the moon?
We wanted only the brash broadside of wind,
only mountain crag & drag of tide.
We wanted only feathers' flash & dolphin smile,
mile upon mile of limb & leaf, fin & fur—
only things forever guileless & guiltless.

We ate the pomegranate of our distress,
& called the owls of our willful & forgotten days.
Would they come—& if they did, would they bear
the gift of names in their beaks?

In the night of saws & brocade & stolen dreams,
where did we look to find a path forward?
Did we seek the genesis of cobalt or iron?
Did the salt of concern narrow the distance
between fear & frankness?

The sea's lungs breathed jasmine & mint.
Fire had its own geography,
snow its own rhythm & tone.
Astronomers read the moon's obituary,

& we learned the wordless habits of dust.
Did we count our breaths on the path,
trying to create a star chart of forgiveness?

On drowsy days, we spent our time
remaking regrets with paper & tire rubber,
with lost pigeon feathers.
Ah, the solace & sincerity of pink parasols
on rain-filled days, as clouds settled into our bodies.

Each moment held its onyx promise,
a luster of frost & impermanence.
Had we touched a red oak bole, a spider web,
or a beating heart, we'd have known something
so pure we'd never doubt it.

Did we seek the insights intrinsic to a cubic meter
of despair? What could be salvaged or saved
from vagabondage or despoliation?
A feral horse veered from all fences,
as, unperturbed, grasshoppers chewed
like little harvesters, & a blue racer
slipknotted through the grass.

Asleep or awake, we lived in permanent aurora,
ceaseless green delirium of words.
Every awakening was a hunger,
& every hunger the beginning of sounds,
the lust of wings for air.

In the room of a dog's bark, we saw pain.
We took note of the flower & its shadow,
the green-burning blurt through soil, the spurt
toward the sun-obscured stars. & we watched,
cell by withered cell, the complete undoing.

Hurricanes bled water into air,
galaxies bled light into space.
Time cut its jugular & bled rust into everything.
Each new day we wrote our names
in the book of anonymity & uncommon myth.

There was forbearance in the moonlight,
calm in the calling of owls.
A raptor glided across our thoughts.
Wings slid black down black-streaked clouds,
& wolves hammered sparks from the heart of night.

Dreamsoul, fabricated of light, the song
whose words we knew at birth & never forgot,
a song like the first & last stars to burn
in the vast blackness. How to comprehend
the scale? In each fingernail a rising sun,
in each dream a night of dreamless sleep.
We wakened into tuneful light
that did not begin & did not end.

Come here, star, we said.
Come say you'll stay longer than we can dream
or hope to stay with you.
Come here, star. Come to the edge
of this moment that will not return—
& burn beyond all time.

Winter Peaches

All my life they've been the things
that have made summer summer.

At the farm, we kept crates of them
in the cool basement shadows.

My brother & I'd run in,
sweating from playing in the sun,

clump down the wood plank stairs,
& we'd each grab a peach

from the paper wrappers & bite
into the sweet, red, wet flesh.

We ate them greedily
& peach juice dripped

down our fingers
& ran down our chins.

Or we'd gorge on a bowl of them,
cut up, sprinkled with sugar,

& immersed in cream.
But this appears to be the year

I do things differently.
So, in the middle of a January

snowstorm, I eat the peaches
Laurie bought just for me,

knowing how much I love them,
I eat them in a bowl,

with honey & Half-And-Half,
& they are sweet,

sweeter even than memory.

Thanksgiving Song

I can sing with the broken bone
of the yellow half-moon. I can dream
with the phosphor sunrise of joy.

Grapevine, grizzly, starfish, hairstreak
Butterfly. Each thing speaks its name,
& more. Larkspur, salamander, squid,

tangerine. Each name sings
light needles into ebony dusk.
Blackbirds flock by, fly up—ink

wrinkling on sky's blue page. I take
breath exhaled from a sea otter's nose,
listen to catfish turn in the river's

dark dungeon. Who can bear
the pure flames of a mourning dove's
heart—ultramarine & gold?

Who can taste, without original fear,
the honeybees' starry nectar?
The tree frog deserves gratitude.

Horned owl & muskrat deserve
thanksgiving. As do red wolf,
mule deer, armadillo, & coral snake.

We can never sing enough, never utter
sufficiently our gratitude, not even
if our lives were one continuous prayer

of thanksgiving, because we are all,
yes, each & every one, the last,
least, best, unexpected thing.

Notes

The Hayden epigraph is from "Bahá'u'lláh in the Garden of Ridwan."

"Family Separation": The title refers to the Trump Administration's policy—begun in April 2018 and suspended in June 2018—of detaining undocumented immigrants for prosecution and separating them from their children, who were held in facilities managed by the U.S. Department of Health and Human Services. This policy was almost universally condemned by individuals and by organizations such as the American Psychiatric Association, the American Academy of Pediatrics, and the American College of Physicians. The American Academy of Pediatrics said the policy would cause "irreparable harm" to the interned children.

"Fugue for the Sandy Hook Dead": The Sandy Hook Elementary School shooting took place on 14 December 2012. Twenty children age six and seven were slain, as were six members of the school staff.

"The Sea Anemone Must Wed Lightning" and "When Dreams Become Porous": In Zoroastrianism, paradise is referred to as the House of Song. Hell is referred to as the House of Lies.

"Knocking the Stars Senseless": This poem's context is the series of shootings that occurred over eleven days in the cities listed. Alton Sterling was shot by police in Baton Rouge on July 6, 2016; Philando Castile was shot by police in St. Paul on July 7; five police officers were killed and seven were wounded in a shooting in Dallas on July 8; three police officers were killed and three were wounded in a shooting in Baton Rouge on July 17.

"For García Lorca": For more information on Lorca's death, Ian Gibson's accounts in *The Assassination of Federico García Lorca* and in his biography, *Federico García Lorca*, are both authoritative and affecting.

Acknowledgments

I am grateful to the editors of these magazines in the United States and England, in whose pages versions of these poems appeared, sometimes under different titles:

Bacopa Literary Review: "After the Political Speeches"

The Bellwether: "Fugue for the Sandy Hook Dead" (as "The Stars' Black Anodyne of Sleep"; reprinted in another version under the new title in *Bullets Into Bells*)

By&By Poetry: "Broken Bells"

envy's sting: "The Otter" (reprinted in *Anthology of Magazine Verse and Yearbook of American Poetry*)

Evergreen Review: "Darkfall"; "Fugue: Assassins and the Dead"; "Lorca's Gypsies at Auschwitz" (as "Gypsies at Auschwitz"); "The Sea Anemone Must Wed Lightning"

Indicia: "When Dreams Become Porous"

The New Guard: "Knocking the Stars Senseless" (finalist for the Knightville Poetry Contest)

Orbis: "The Sunlight Was Mortal" (Reader's Choice Award)

Provincetown Magazine: "Ballad of the Witch" (Marge Piercy selected "Ballad of the Witch" as the Second Place National Winner in the fourth annual Joe Gouveia Outermost Poetry Contest)

Riverrun: "The Old Crow" (reprinted in *Nebraska Presence: An Anthology of Poetry"*)

Southern Poetry Review: "Day of the Dead" (reprinted in the 10th Anniversary issue)

SPSM&H: "Housework" (award poem, published on the cover)

Wind Magazine: "Kwik Shop Epiphany"

Writers' Journal: "Thanksgiving Song" (as "Praise Song"; First Place Award)

"Gypsies at Auschwitz" was awarded Honorable Mention in the annual *Writer's Digest* Non-rhyming Poetry Contest

"Her Art" appeared in the anthology, *Misbehaving Nebraskans: Writers and Artists Celebrate the State's 150th*.

"For García Lorca," "Housework," "Kwik Shop Epiphany," "October Butterfly," and "The Otter" appeared in the chapbook, *From the Dead Before* (Lone Willow Press).

*****

Some of these poems were written with particular individuals in mind. Others made their dedicatory intentions known after composition:
"The Sea Anemone Must Wed Lightning" is for Aphrodite Avram.
"I Wore the Night Like a Roquelaure" is for Matt Dean.
"The Otter" is for Tony Jasnowski.
"Her Art" is for Cat Dixon.
"Darkfall" is for Mary K. Stillwell.
"Ballad of the Witch" is for Suzanne Kessler and Natasha Kessler-Rains.
"Family Separation" is for Joan Houlihan.
"Skydiving" is for Jeffrey Levine.
"Winter Peaches" is for Twyla Hansen.
"Fugue for the Sandy Hook Dead" is for Lauren Norris Rodgers.
"A Handful of Fireflies" and "Every Awakening Was a Hunger" are for Laurie.
"Subdivision Eclogue" is for Jesse.
"October Butterfly" is for Adrien.
"Housework" is for Vahíd.
"Kwik Shop Epiphany" is for Fred.
"Ghost Music" is dedicated to the memory of my father, Dana Peep.

*****

A deep debt of gratitude is owed to Laurie, the first reader of all of these poems, as well as of numerous versions of this collection; and to Cat Dixon, Laura Madeline Wiseman, Trent Walters, Joan Houlihan, Jeffrey Levine, Matt Dean, and Aphrodite Avram, who read and offered critiques of various versions of this collection (some were so self-sacrificing as to do so multiple times).

I will always be thankful, too, to the members of my writing group, with whom I shared many of these poems: Michelle Brown Lyles, Annemarie Burton Drvol, Katie Berger, Cat Dixon, Sky Dixon, Trent Walters, Fran Higgins, Shyla Punteney, Britny Cordera, Genevieve Williams, Kristen Clanton, Maritza Estrada, Stelaton Mave, Shellie Brown, Chantelle Green, Kellie Marie Hayden, Michael Grove, and Laura Madeline Wiseman.

I also owe hearty thanks to these other clear-eyed and generous readers: Suzanne Kessler, Kandida Lehmann Gebdribm, Natasha Kessler-Rains, Twyla Hansen, Matt Mason, Tony Jasnowski, Shelly Clark Geiser, Mary K. Stillwell, Amy Nejezchleb, Lorraine Duggin, and the late Fredrick Zydek, Needless to say, I alone am responsible for any infelicities that may remain.

Special gratitude to Kimberly Verhines, Jerri Bourrous, and the Stephen F. Austin State University Press.

CPSIA information can be obtained
at www.ICGtesting.com
Printed in the USA
LVHW041925181119
637699LV00007B/1435